Sermons On The Second Readings

For Sundays After Pentecost (Last Third)

A New Resolve

Scott Suskovic

A NEW RESOLVE
PENTECOST: LAST THIRD

Copyright © 2009 by
CSS Publishing Company, Inc.
Lima, Ohio

All rights reserved. No part of this publication may be reproduced in any manner whatsoever without the prior permission of the publisher, except in the case of brief quotations embodied in critical articles and reviews. Inquiries should be addressed to: Permissions, CSS Publishing Company, Inc., 517 South Main Street, Lima, Ohio 45804.

Some scripture quotations are from the New Revised Standard Version of the Bible, copyright 1989 by the Division of Christian Education of the National Council of the Churches of Christ in the USA. Used by permission.

Some scripture quotations are from the Holy Bible, New Living Translation, copyright © 1996. Used by permission of Tyndale House Publishers, Inc., Wheaton, Illinois 60189. All rights reserved.

Some scripture quotations are from the Revised Standard Version of the Bible, copyrighted 1946, 1952 ©, 1971, 1973, by the Division of Christian Education of the National Council of the Churches of Christ in the USA. Used by permission.

For more information about CSS Publishing Company resources, visit our website at www.csspub.com or email us at custserv@csspub.com or call (800) 241-4056.

Cover design by Barbara Spencer

ISSN: 1937-1454

ISBN-13: 978-0-7880-2657-7
ISBN-10: 0-7880-2657-7

PRINTED IN USA

Table Of Contents

**Sermons For Sundays
After Pentecost (Last Third)
A New Resolve
by Scott Suskovic**

Proper 23
 Pentecost 21
 Ordinary Time 28
   Living In Chains
   2 Timothy 2:8-15
	5

Proper 24
 Pentecost 22
 Ordinary Time 29
   The Word Alone
   2 Timothy 3:14—4:5
	11

Proper 25
 Pentecost 23
 Ordinary Time 30
   Endurance
   2 Timothy 4:6-8, 16-18
	17

Reformation Day
   Saint And Sinner
   Romans 3:19-28
	23

All Saints   29
    The Final Word
    Ephesians 1:11-23

Proper 26   35
Pentecost 24
Ordinary Time 31
    Worthy Of Your Call
    2 Thessalonians 1:1-4, 11-12

Proper 27   39
Pentecost 25
Ordinary Time 32
    Sarah
    2 Thessalonians 2:1-5, 13-17

Proper 28   45
Pentecost 26
Ordinary Time 33
    No Work, No Food!
    2 Thessalonians 3:6-13

Christ The King   49
Proper 29
    This Is A King?
    Colossians 1:11-20

Thanksgiving Day   55
    A New Resolve
    Philippians 4:4-9

Lectionary Preaching After Pentecost   61

US/Canadian Lectionary Comparison   63

Proper 23
Pentecost 21
Ordinary Time 28
2 Timothy 2:8-15

Living In Chains

"... suffer as I do" (2 Timothy 1:12).

It was in 1965 that the Rolling Stones recorded the song, "I Can't Get No Satisfaction." Even today, over forty years later, we are still saying the same words and feeling the same emptiness of trying and trying, but getting no satisfaction. Commercials promise it with whiter teeth and fresher breath. Wall Street promises it with higher returns. Soap operas promise it with a dynamic love life. Yet those who have conquered each of those summits come up with the same cry, "I can't get no satisfaction." Can you?

Contentment is a rare gift that comes through a deep, personal relationship with Jesus that transcends circumstances. It flows from a sure and certain hope that because Jesus lives, I will, too. Neither death nor life nor things present nor things to come will separate me from the love of God in Christ Jesus. In that promise, we find that rare gift of contentment, peace, and patience.

Whenever I read Paul's prison letter, I marvel at the peace and patience in his tone.

> *And because I preach this good news, I am suffering and have been chained like a criminal. But the word of God cannot be chained. I am willing to endure anything if it will bring salvation and eternal glory in Christ Jesus....* — 2 Timothy 2:9-10 (NLT)

Why isn't Paul lashing out against his unjust imprisonment? Why isn't he condemning those who arrested him? Why isn't he furiously scribbling out threats of revenge? I've always marveled at the peace and patience found in Paul's prison letters probably because I would have been far less graceful. There is truly a peace that passes all human understanding in these words, even while Paul was living in chains. It flows from a rare gift of peace and contentment.

In the 1730s and 1740s, Jonathan Edwards nearly single-handedly led the spiritual awakening in America. He is known best for his sermon, "Sinners in the Hands of an Angry God." However, there was one jealous pastor in town who took displeasure to Edwards' popularity and spread nasty rumors about this preacher. At first, no one took the rumors seriously. After all, this was Jonathan Edwards we were talking about. And then, as the rumors persisted, some asked Edwards about their validity. He refused to comment, which created even more gossip. His silence created even more controversy until finally the townspeople confronted Edwards and asked him to either confirm or deny the charges. Edwards still refused to comment saying that he would rather trust God to vindicate him than to rely on his own eloquence in defense.

Edwards displayed the same kind of peace and patience that Paul had while living in chains. While many of us would have sought revenge or at least cried out, "I can't get no satisfaction!" Edwards echoed the patience and peace of Paul when taking the higher ground. Paul wrote, "If we die with him, we will also live with him. If we endure hardship, we will reign with him" (2 Timothy 2:11-12).

When it comes to this kind of peace and patience, the Bible refers to two different kinds. The first is dealing with circumstances.

> *Be patient, therefore, beloved, until the coming of the Lord ... you have heard of the endurance of Job, and you have seen the purpose of the Lord, how the Lord is compassionate and merciful.* — James 5:7a, 11b

You've heard of the patience of Job. This was a patience of circumstance. Job wasn't angry at anyone in particular. His family was killed. His herds were lost. His home was destroyed and he was covered with sores. There was no one to get mad at, per se. He needed patience with the circumstance. This kind of patience is inspired by hope. Brighter days lay ahead because God is God and I am his. Job said, "I know that my redeemer lives and at the last when my flesh has been destroyed, then from my flesh I shall see God." Paul and Edwards shared that same hope in the midst of horrendous circumstances.

The second kind of peace and patience is with people. It is a patience not inspired by hope but rather with mercy. Let me explain. When I go to the hospital to be with someone whose loved one has died tragically, there is sadness, there is anger, there are questions, and sometimes it is all directed at me — "Why did this happen, pastor?" I know that they are not angry with me. I don't respond harshly and take offense. I respond as you would — with patience inspired by mercy. When you talk to a friend or a family member and it feels like you are being attacked, sometimes you just have to ask, "Is this really about me or is there something going on in her life ... and right now, I just need to take it. I'm not going to get upset or walk away but right now, I'm going to be patient because right now she needs mercy."

Sitting in prison, living in chains, Paul shows patience with his captors. They were not to blame. They were following orders. Edwards, on the other hand, showed patience with his accuser who was not following orders. In fact, he had malicious intent! But as Paul Harvey would say, here is the rest of the story of Jonathan Edwards. Unfortunately, the crowd eventually believed the rumors concerning Edwards, defrocked him, and kicked him out of town. He remained in exile for eight years until the other pastor, humbled by Edwards' example of mercy, stepped forward, and confessed that it was all a lie.

Now what? I understand that I, as a mature Christian, am not to seek revenge. *Vengeance is mine, says the Lord.* Why am I banned from seeking revenge? Because with my dark, sinful heart, I will never be content on just evening the score with my enemy. I'll go overboard. I'll get one up on him. I'll ... I'll.... You get the picture. You see why revenge is forbidden — because I can't be trusted with a tied game.

But what about vindication? What about being exonerated? What about correcting a lie? Martin Luther stood before the trial of his life, the Diet of Worms in 1521, and said, "Show me by reason and by scripture that I am a heretic and I'll be the first to throw my books on the fire." He wasn't silent. He took a stand. Where do we draw that line from patience to being a doormat in which you become walked upon, disregarded, and abused?

I don't know. I confess, I don't know. It is a razor-thin line at times. But let me share with you an image that came to me this past week. My ten-year-old son, Nathan, and I do this thing periodically, in which I'll tell him to, for example, clean up his room.

If he is in one of those moods, he'll say, "No."

I'll say a bit more firmly, "Clean up your room."

And more defiantly he says, "NO."

Squaring off to him, I say, "Now."

Facing me he says, "Nope." (Now you need to picture this with the two of us barely keeping a straight face.)

I'll take off my jacket, roll up my sleeves and say, "You know I can make you, don't you?"

He'll face me, drop his baseball, take off his jacket, and with a barely concealed smirk says, "No you can't."

Then I wrestle him to the carpet, pin him to the ground, get a couple of playful jabs in his belly, put him in a half nelson and when he says, "Uncle!" I say again, "Now, clean up your room. Please."

And he says, "Okay."

I have the power. Until he turns sixteen anyway, I have the power. I can choose to use it or I can choose patience. Can you image what would have happened if Jesus had argued at his trial? Can you imagine Jesus talking theology with the high priest or ethics with the temple guards or the essence of the messianic prophecies with the council? Who would you have put your money on? Who would have "won"? But he didn't. He had the power but he chose patience. He also had the power to call down legions of angels to defend him, restore him, and punish those false accusers. But he didn't. He had the power. He chose patience.

Where is that line drawn between patience and becoming a doormat that is walked upon, taken advantage of, and abused? I don't know. It's there, somewhere, I just not sure where. I do know that the answer is found in the extraordinary patience that God has shown me.

His conversation with me goes something like this. "Clean up your life."
"No."
"Stop doubting me."
"Can't."
"No more questions, and I mean it."
"Sorry, nope"
"I can make you."
"No you can't."

And sometimes, *sometimes* God has to get a little rough with me to make his point but always with patience and not with power.

If I am filled with his Spirit, then it is his peace in me that I work for in others and it is his patience with me that I extend to others, much like Paul living in chains or Edwards living with false accusations. How can I dare hold back from others the love, the forgiveness, the peace, and the patience that I have received from God? Amen.

**Proper 24
Pentecost 22
Ordinary Time 29
2 Timothy 3:14—4:5**

The Word Alone

"All scripture is inspired by God" (2 Timothy 3:16).

There was a woman who called her pastor late one night in a panic and said, "Pastor, quickly, tell me what I believe." Another believer from a different church who challenged her about her beliefs had cornered her. She quickly found that she could not articulate the basic teachings of her church. "Pastor, quickly, tell me what I believe."

There may be more than one person gathering in worship this morning who, if hard pressed, may be less than clear about what they believe. Are you one?

Where does one start in establishing a baseline for belief? Church doctrine? Parental teaching? The local pastor? Inner instinct?

For those coming from the Protestant Reformation, that baseline can only be scripture. From this sixteenth-century movement came the battle cry, "the word alone." Our baseline for what we believe must flow from the word alone. One of the many texts used to support this teaching and belief of the centrality of scripture is 2 Timothy 3. Let's look at that text again.

> But as for you, continue in what you have learned and firmly believed, knowing from whom you learned it, and how from childhood you have known the sacred writings that are able to instruct you for salvation through faith in Christ Jesus. All scripture is inspired by God

> *and useful for teaching, for reproof, for correction, and for training in righteousness, so that everyone who belongs to God may be proficient, equipped for every good work.* — 2 Timothy 3:14-17

Let's take that apart. The word "inspired" is a unique word. This is the only time it occurs in the New Testament. It refers to wisdom that comes from God, or quite literally, God's Spirit has been infused or breathed upon it. Therefore, more than just the creative thoughts or opinion of some authors writing on papyrus, scripture has a unique divine authority unlike any other writing.

That authority, that power, is shown in what God's word accomplishes. It inspired faith with a wisdom that transcends human knowledge. It teaches, reproofs, and corrects. It trains people in righteousness, equipping them for every good work. The power and the authority of scripture are found in what it does.

Luther knew this to be true. He knew and firmly believed that all theories, all theologies, all teachings are to be tested against the teachings of the Bible. If they contradict the teachings of the Bible, they are to be refused. If they are in agreement with the teachings of the Bible, they are to be followed ... come what may.

This firm belief and stance on the authority and inspiration of the Bible came to the ultimate test in 1521 when Luther was called on the carpet to denounce his books and his teachings. For months, Luther's books were being burned in Rome until finally the Pope ordered Luther to appear before a council in the city of Worms, Germany.

Make no mistake. This was a serious offense. If found guilty of heresy, Luther, a 38-year-old German monk, could not only be kicked out of the church but also be put to death. There was a lot on the line not only in Luther's life but also for the future of the Reformation.

For hours they went round and round, each side selecting their words carefully until, at the end, the interrogator looked at Luther and said, "Martin Luther, the teachings found in your book have been declared to be in error with the church. I ask you for the last time, do you recant your teachings or are you willing to bear the consequences?"

This is where the Hollywood version of things makes the reality fuzzy. The image that prevails is one of a tall Luther, defying the wicked and corrupt Roman structure, pounding his fist on the table, clutching a Bible and yelling, "Here I stand!" Then he mounts a white horse and begins the Reformation. That is the image you may have seen of Luther looking far off with a large Bible in his hands — defiant, confident, strong.

That's not what happened.

When he was asked for the last time to recant, Luther said in a voice that was barely audible, "Give me 24 hours." The magnitude of the moment as this 38-year-old German monk was telling the church that it had been wrong for centuries and that he alone bore the flame of truth almost came crashing down on him.

That night, in the solitude of his room, Luther wrote one of the most moving prayers ever written. It was his own time in the Garden of Gethsemane.

> *O God, Almighty God everlasting! How dreadful is the world! Behold how its mouth opens to swallow me up, and how small is my faith in Thee! ... Oh! the weakness of the flesh, and the power of Satan! If I am to depend upon any strength of this world — all is over ... Help me against all the wisdom of this world ... The work is not mine, but Thine. I have no business here ... I have nothing to contend for with these great men of the world! I would gladly pass my days in happiness and peace. But the cause is Thine ... And it is righteous and everlasting! O Lord! Help me! O faithful and unchangeable God! Do you not hear? My God. Are you no longer living? You have chosen me for this work. I know it ... Therefore, O God, accomplish your own will!*
>
> *Lord — where are you? Come, I pray. Behold, I am prepared to lay down my life for your truth. For the cause is holy. It is your own. I will not let you go. Though the world should be thronged with devils and this body should be cast forth, trodden under foot, cut in pieces, consumed to ashes, my soul is thine. O God, help me.... Amen.*[1]

The next morning, Luther returned to the courtroom to resume testimony. The prosecutor continued. "I ask you, Martin, for the last time — answer candidly and without horns — do you or do you not repudiate your books and the errors which they contain?"

In words of desperation, knowing there was no way to escape the inevitable, a tired and worn Luther replied not with defiance but with a sense of exhaustion, "Since then your Majesty and your lordships desire a simply reply, I will answer without horns and without teeth. Unless I am convinced by scripture and plain reason — I do not accept the authority of popes and councils, for they have contradicted each other — my conscience is captive to the word of God. I cannot and I will not recant anything, for to go against conscience is neither right nor safe. Here I stand, I cannot do otherwise. God help me."

It wasn't a matter of being stubborn. It wasn't an issue of having a grand vision of a Reformation. It wasn't the goal of having a church named after him. This was not movement fueled by an out-of-control ego.

It's about believing and trusting God's word — not a part of it — not selected sections that are to my advantage. It's about not dismissing those parts that make you squirm — the whole ball of wax — the entire package. It's about trusting and believing that God's word alone has the power and authority it claims.

- The word alone is the final authority for teaching, reproof, correcting, and training. It is the lamp unto our feet. It is inspired by God.
- It claims that I am saved not by my works or how much I give or how much I do or how often I attend. I am saved by my faith alone in Jesus Christ as my Lord.
- It claims that this salvation is never earned. Indeed everyone has fallen short of the glory of God. All deserve God's wrath. But instead, we receive not what we deserve but what God in his mercy wants to give ... his grace alone.
- It claims that everyone has been gifted by God with different talents, and God calls each as individuals to identify those

gifts, develop those gifts, and use those gifts in the body of Christ as a part of the priesthood of all believers.
- It claims that that Word of God became flesh in Jesus and dwelt among us full of grace and truth.

Following his interrogation at Worms, Luther translated the Bible into German and put it into the hands of all the German peasants. He did this under penalty of death because he was convinced that one German peasant armed with scripture is more powerful than 1,000 cardinals and bishops and popes without it. Clergy do not have a corner on the market because they are clergy. That truth comes from the word alone in the hands of any believer.

Here I stand. Amen.

---

1. Martin Luther, *Luther's Prayers* (Minneapolis, Augsburg, 1994).

**Proper 25
Pentecost 23
Ordinary Time 30
2 Timothy 4:6-8, 16-18**

Endurance

*I have fought the good fight, I have finished the race, I
have kept the faith.* — 2 Timothy 4:7

When my daughter, Hannah, was five years old we lived in Minnesota. Before she entered kindergarten, she had to take an entrance exam. Being the non-competitive but responsible parent that I am, I decided to help Hannah prepare for this test. I taught her how to count to ten — in four languages. I taught her the colors by buying a box of crayons — 64 count, including turquoise, magenta, and chartreuse. We worked on a puzzle of the United States with each individual state cut out so we could learn the names, location, and capital of all fifty. After six months of cramming, I felt she was ready for her entrance exam. My wife took her to the test and then phoned me with the results. Do you know what? They didn't ask her to count to ten in Japanese. She wasn't asked the capital of Wyoming. But she was asked, "What's this?" And they pointed to her shoulder. "What's this?" And they pointed to her hand. "What this?" And they pointed to a part of her body that she had never seen, had no idea what it was, and had to shrug her shoulders. It was her elbow. I had forgotten to teach her what an elbow was. Thankfully, she was still allowed into kindergarten.

I'm still doing this cramming today as Hannah is preparing for graduation from high school and getting ready for college. Can you do laundry? Can you manage finances? Do you know how to make grandma's special sauce? You want them to do well and be ready. These are things they should know. There are things we should all know whether it is entering kindergarten or college. On the top of that list is endurance.

What do you wish you hadn't quit? College? Do you wish you would have finished that degree? How about the piano? Do you wish you had not stopped those lessons? What about exercise? Did you give up too early? What about a job that would have led to something or a hobby that once brought you great pleasure? What do you wish you hadn't quit? A marriage? Do you wish you would have tried harder? What about God? Maybe you gave up on God long ago — stopped praying, stopped believing, and now you are just going through the motions. What do you wish you hadn't quit?

Why did you quit? We all know the answer. It's the same reason we all quit. Because it was easy to quit. You didn't like taking tests so you quit college and got a job. You would rather go out and play with your friends than practice the piano. It was easier to walk out on the marriage than to sit down with that person and work it out. It was easier to sleep in on Sunday, read the paper, and drink a cup of coffee than to get the children up, fight the parking, and come to church. Come on, let's be honest. It's a whole lot easier to be a quitter.

I bet if you were to ask successful people about the secret to their success, one quality that would be consistent among them all would be endurance. In many cases, instead of taking the easy way, looking for shortcuts, or wanting instant success, they didn't quit. They were willing to delay gratification by making a conscious decision to endure the pain now in order to receive a greater reward later.

Many people, however, are wired differently. I'm told that there is a small box at Bell Laboratories. The box has one switch. When you turn the switch on, a skeleton hand comes out, reaches over, and turns itself off. That's all it does. It's wired to turn itself off. A lot of people are that way — wired to quit. At the first sight of hardship, at the first hint that this will take time, I'll just turn myself off. No endurance. It's just easier to quit

How do you find endurance? When you are at that quitting point, how do you move forward? When you are running the marathon and your body is screaming to quit; when your boss is a tyrant and you hate your job; when you've got one more exam, one more paper, and you are just spent; when you are having the same argument with your spouse for the twentieth time and you are getting nowhere; or when you've been praying for so long and haven't received so much as a whisper from God. How do you break through those quitting points when it would be a whole lot easier just to cash in, walk away, and quit?

For that, I want to turn to a favorite passage of mine in 2 Timothy 4:7. Paul is in prison awaiting his execution. He knows that the time of his death is soon. He has time to reflect on his life and writes with the deep contentment of one who has had endurance: "I have fought the good fight, I have finished the race, I have kept the faith."

Do you hear the contentment? Do you sense words of accomplishment? At the end of his life, Paul has no regrets. That would be great, wouldn't it? But you know that there were times Paul thought about quitting.

> *Five different times the Jewish leaders gave me thirty-nine lashes. Three times I was beaten with rods. Once I was stoned. Three times I was shipwrecked. Once I spent a whole night and a day adrift at sea. I have traveled on many long journeys. I have faced danger from rivers and from robbers. I have faced danger from my own people, the Jews, as well as from the Gentiles. I have faced danger in the cities, in the deserts, and on the seas. And I have faced danger from men who claim to be believers but are not. I have worked hard and long, enduring many sleepless nights. I have been hungry and thirsty and have often gone without food. I have shivered in the cold, without enough clothing to keep me warm.*
> — 2 Corinthians 11:24-27 (NLT)

How many times do you have to be tied to a pole and beaten to within an inch of your life until you call it quits? How many times do you have to be shipwrecked before you think, "There has to be an easier way"? How many times do you have to go hungry, be thirsty or cold, and say, "I am so out of here"? You know Paul thought about quitting often. But he didn't. He endured. Before he died, he left us with three keys to his endurance.

Fight The Good Fight

It wasn't just any fight. It was the good fight. It was a fight worth fighting. There are a lot of things we fight for, most of it is for pride and ego and greed. Those are not good fights. What is?

I'm thinking about an alcoholic I know who struggles each day wanting a drink but has not taken one for the past nineteen years — he fights the good fight. I'm thinking about the lawyer in our church who adopted some children. To give them the time they need, she gave up her practice — she fights the good fight. I know a couple who have reasons to go their separate ways but choose to do the hard job of making it work, every day — they fight the good fight. I'm thinking about the person who has lost a child, one of the greatest fears of a parent, yet comes here every Sunday to praise, thank, and worship God — he fights the good fight. I'm thinking about the college students with many opportunities to wander, many opportunities to slack off, and many opportunities to make bad choices when others around them seem to major in trouble — but they don't. They fight the good fight. Paul says here, decide right now what is good, what is important, what is worth having, and then choose to fight the good fight.

Finish The Race

There are plenty of people willing to start something — start a relationship, start a job, start an exercise program, or start a program. Starting is not the problem. It's finishing the race that takes endurance.

Problem is, Hollywood glamorizes quitters. Have you ever noticed how often on television or in the movies, the boss demands one more project, the tension builds, the music crescendos until finally the worker explodes, yells, "I quit," and slams the door and the crowd cheers? Wouldn't that be great? I want to have that moment with the drama, the music, with that flare. Or the marriage that explodes with nasty words, clothes thrown out the window, and a dagger in the back — that's the way I would like to leave, with a scene. Or the college student who is overwhelmed so he blows it off, parties, and we think that looks a whole lot more fun than the library. Hollywood glamorizes the quitter who has no endurance. They focus on that exhilarating moment — "I quit." They don't show the worker now in the third month of being unemployed and staring at an eviction notice. They don't show the fallout and pain from a broken home. They don't show the college student kicked out of school and now flipping burgers and drinking his way through the weekend.

Paul begins by saying that this is a good fight, something worth the hardship. Now finish it. Finish the race. Finish strong. How? By being a person of faith.

Keep The Faith

This one is hard, isn't it? Keeping the faith in the midst of the storm. Keeping your trust even when you think you are walking this path alone. Keep the faith. Let me be honest with you, this is difficult. I think of my ministry when the demands are so high and I think, "Am I the right person for this job?" It would be easier to not to finish. It would be easy to lose faith.

How many times did Jesus think about quitting? — when they pulled his beard, sunk thorns into his scalp, beat him, and nailed spikes through his hands and feet. How many times did he think, "I can't do this. I want to quit. Surely there has to be an easier way, God, than this."

But he didn't. He endured. He fought the good fight — and what made it good and worthwhile was you. You were worth the fight. He finished the race — the last words he breathed on this earth were, "It is finished." And he kept the faith — "Father, into your hands I commit my soul."

Endurance is something even more important than knowing that this is an elbow. It means to fight the good fight, finish the race, keep the faith. Why? For the prize; delaying gratification now for even greater pleasure in the future. Paul always had the end in mind. He wanted the prize. He wrote, "The crown of righteousness that the Lord, the righteous judge will give me on that great day of his return." Then he looks right at you and adds, "And the prize is not just for me, but for all who eagerly look forward to his glorious return." Endurance is more than just sticking to it — it's keeping your eye on the prize. Amen.

**Reformation Day
Romans 3:19-28**

Saint And Sinner

"Since all have sinned and fall short of the glory of God" (Romans 3:23).

In the mid-1920s there was a successful, young, stockbroker who made it big on Wall Street. Really big! He had it all, materially speaking; money, country club membership, wealthy friends. He also drank. A lot! When the crash hit in 1929 and lasted for several years, he lost everything ... except his bottle of gin. His wife had to go to work only to come home day after day exhausted to find her husband drunk on the couch again.

He tried many times to stop drinking but couldn't until, with the help of a friend who had himself overcome the bottle with strong spiritual guidance, this young stockbroker, Bill W., began a process known today as the 12-step approach. Today, millions have found sobriety through this organization co-founded by Bill W. known as Alcoholics Anonymous.

Though it is not a blatantly religious movement, AA is grounded in some very basic spiritual or religious tenets beginning with a strong belief that God is the only help to achieve sobriety.

Step one begins the process by admitting that you are powerless over alcohol and that God is your only strength. This first step is critical and one of the most difficult. What you are saying is that alcohol has taken control of your life, and you cannot fix this problem yourself. After this, additional steps include making an honest inventory of your life and confessing these sins to another person.

I have had the opportunity to attend a few AA meetings as I have accompanied parishioners to meetings for the first time for support and encouragement. You will never find a more honest group of people because, as they told me, an alcoholic is a great liar but one drunk cannot lie to another. They know all the lies, all the excuses, all the lines. Honesty is the only alternative.

The meetings begin with introductions. First names only, like Bill W., and with the same lines. "Hello, I'm Susan and I'm an alcoholic. I have been sober since May 3, 1988."

Did you catch that? She hasn't had a drink in over twenty years — dry, sober, alcohol-free. And yet, what did she say? "I'm Susan, I *used* to be an alcoholic? I'm a *recovering* or *recovered* alcoholic?" No, the reality is, "I'm Susan and I am an alcoholic."

Is Susan free from alcohol or is she still in its grips? On the one hand, Susan is 100% free from the grips of alcohol. She is sober, dry, and alcohol-free. By the grace of God and the power of the Holy Spirit, she has been transformed. On the other hand, she is still in bondage to the condition of alcoholism because one drink will start the downward spiral all over again.

The answer is both. She is free and she is enslaved.

Our modern-day understanding of alcoholism is the best example I know to explain an important teaching that flowed from the Reformation called, "Saint and Sinner." Indeed, this teaching is a cornerstone on which is built our entire teaching of grace and faith. Basically, the question is this: Are we free from sin, released from its grips by the power of Christ's death and resurrection, or are we still in bondage to sin and under its demise?

Like the struggle with alcoholism, the answer is both. We are, at the same time, saints and sinners.

Luther spoke and wrote often about this paradoxical condition of the believer. On the one hand, we are 100% saints — the shackles of death have been destroyed by the blood of Jesus. Paul writes in Galatians, "For freedom Christ has set you free; stand fast, therefore, and do not submit again to a yoke of slavery." In Romans, Paul writes, "... you have been set free from sin" (6:22). "For the law of the Spirit of life in Christ Jesus has set you free from the law of sin and of death" (8:2). We are born again through faith. Death has no power over us. The law no longer rules us. We are 100% saints through our faith in Jesus.

Yet, at the same time, we are 100% sinners in bondage to this condition called sin. Look closely at the reading for today, "For there is no distinction, since all have sinned and fall short of the glory of God" (Romans 3:22b-23). In Romans 3:9-10, "All people ... are under the power of sin. None is righteous — not even one." Unable to completely cast off our sinful nature, we are, in our heart of hearts, a rebel, fleeing from God, spitting apple into his face and declaring, "I am the captain of my own vessel. I am accountable to no one. Just let me be."

When it comes to the condition of sin, we all are addicted. We are all rebels in our hearts. Luther said that it was like the birds of winter. Those that do not fly south try to gather up morsels here and there to survive until spring. Luther went out to feed the birds in his backyard once and instead of coming to him and receive the food, what did they do? They flew away. Pointing at the birds, Luther said, "That's me! God comes to me with goodness, life, and blessings to give and instead of eagerly accepting what God has, I fly away. I'll die without God's help but I am filled with doubt, overcome with fear and wickedly stubborn. God only wants to help and save and I flutter away."

In the *Lutheran Book of Worship*, the confession has these striking words that capture our addiction to sin. *I confess that I am in bondage to sin and cannot free myself.* Bondage — that word refers to that rebellious side that joins Adam and Eve in taking that bite of apple and wanting desperately to become like God. Though we are a saint through our faith in Jesus, that sinner inside keeps us in bondage to sin and we cannot free ourselves.

Is there any hope for us? Any hope at all? I think our best hope is to follow the steps laid out by Alcoholics Anonymous. It has saved millions of people. It works. But do you know what? Just between you and me, it's not new. Even in 1935 when it was founded, they actually stole the idea. It's from the Bible. It is the simple plan of salvation reduced to some easy-to-follow steps. It works for alcohol and, more importantly, it works for this bondage we call sin.

Step One: Admit that you are powerless over sin. Let's take off the mask. Let's stop playing games. Let's no longer pretend we are actually nice people and God is going to grade on a curve. I may not be perfect, I may not be a Mother Teresa, but compared to the other people I know, I am pretty decent. Nonsense! Stop the lies. Each one of us silently jingles in our pockets the nails from the cross. I put him there. I nailed him there. I crucified Jesus. I am powerless over sin.

Step Two: Turn your life over to God. For if there is any hope for me, any hope at all beyond the grave, it will not come from me. I cannot get myself out of this box, this hole, this hell — I need to be lifted out from a power outside of me. Turn your life over to God.

Step Three: Come clean. In your own heart, in your own quiet time, make an honest inventory of your life — who you've wronged, what you've done, how you've messed up — everything. List it all. Don't edit it. Leave in the swear words. After it is completed, add some more.

There is a great story about how Luther dealt with this long list of sins. Evidently, one night he had a nightmare in which the devil took out this huge book full of Luther's sins. They were itemized, numbered, and dated. The sheer size and numbers were overwhelming. The weight of the sins drove Luther to his knees in despair. As the devil completed his evidence against a nervous and contrite Luther, Luther suddenly realized something and said, "You forgot a few." With that he added more and more to the list provided by the devil and then wrote on the bottom, "Paid in full by Jesus Christ."

Step Three is to come clean. Make a list. A long list. Add a couple of more things and then nail it to the cross and walk away. Your debt has been paid in full through the blood of Jesus.

In my last church there was a very active member named Tom. Since he was a member of the council, I made it a point to visit with him in his home. During the course of our talk, he pulled out a coin from his pocket and showed me it. In the center was a big number twenty. He said, "I took my last drink twenty years ago. I'm an alcoholic."

"How did you manage to stay sober?" I asked.

"AA, and by the grace of God," he said.

"Twenty years. That's a long time," I said.

Tom replied, "I don't think of it as twenty years. It is one day at a time. My goal each morning when I get up is to make it through that day without a drink. One day at a time."

That's not only good AA talk but is also good Reformation theology. For Luther knew that this struggle between being a saint and a sinner is a daily battle. He called believers to wage war every morning. Wake up each day with a prayer and the sign of the cross as a means of confessing that sinful nature before God and then, at the same time, receive that forgiveness and recommit yourself that day to walking as a saint in the freedom of the gospel. One day at a time.

When Paul laid out the reality that all have sinned and fall short of the glory of God, it was not meant to be the final word. These words are only the vehicle that moves us forward to hear what we celebrate on this Reformation Day:

> *[We] are now justified by his grace as a gift, through the redemption that is in Christ Jesus ... because in his divine forbearance he had passed over the sins ... for we hold that a person is justified by faith apart from the works prescribed by the law.*
> — Romans 3:24, 25, 28

It all begins today with the very first step. Hello, my name is Scott, and I am a sinner who is in bondage to sin and cannot free myself. But thanks be to God who has called me through the gospel, enlightened me by the Spirit, and who has set me free as a saint through the cross of Jesus Christ.

Thanks be to God! Amen.

All Saints
Ephesians 1:11-23

The Final Word

... we, who were the first to set our hope on Christ, might live for the praise of his glory.
— Ephesians 1:12

Several years ago, I was asked to perform a funeral for a brother of a member of our church. I'll call him Jason. When I don't know the person, I usually gather the family together and ask them about their most vivid memories of the person. Most of the time, the next hour is filled with laughter and tears and fond memories.

When I asked Jason's family about their memories, there was this awkward pause. It was as if they knew what they were supposed to say, but they couldn't say it. They knew they were supposed to say that Jason would have given the shirt off his back to a stranger. They knew they were supposed to say that Jason never said a bad word about anyone. They knew they were supposed to say that Jason had love for his family and loyalty to his friends. Only they couldn't say it. It didn't fit. It wasn't true.

Finally one of the family members broke the awkward silence said, "Jason had made many bad choices, burned a lot of bridges, and hurt a lot of feelings. The stories, images, and memories that we have just couldn't be shared at a funeral sermon."

Funerals bring with them a myriad of emotions — sadness, loneliness, anger, hurt feelings, and unresolved guilt. Most of it remains unspoken.

What do you say at a funeral? It's often awkward, isn't it? The soft smiles and hushed tones. The repetitive phrases, "I'm so sorry for your loss. He was a good man. Good to see you. I wish it were under better circumstances." It's awkward, so you kick the ground, adjust the tie, hold a cup of coffee, or don't say anything at all.

I've been to many funerals. Sometimes the preacher feels as if he must entertain us with off-color stories and funny events. At other times, the words are so flattering that you are sure that the deceased is on the fast track to canonization next to Mother Teresa. Sometimes, they don't know what to say and so they just talk ... just talk and fill the void with words. What do you say at a funeral?

In John 11, Jesus attended a funeral. He got there late — four days late. Didn't matter, though. They were waiting for him. They wanted him there, desperately. They wanted him to say something comforting, something meaningful. Surely Jesus will have something to say at this funeral. After all, Lazarus was a friend of Jesus — as well as his sisters, Mary and Martha. If anyone would have just the right words to say to take away the pain, bring comfort, and get life back on track, it would be Jesus. When he arrives, there is a sigh of relief.

Before Jesus could speak, Martha's the first to break the silence with words of accusation, "Lord, if you had been here, my brother would not have died" (John 11:21). Do you hear all the questions in this accusation?

"I don't understand. Help me make sense of this one, Jesus. You were two miles away. Why weren't you here? Why did my brother have to die?"

At every funeral there is a Martha who is seeking answers to difficult questions.

Jesus replied by reminding her that her brother would live again. But Martha seems to pass off those words as meaningless, pie-in-the-sky, sweet nothing, church talk better left for a Hallmark™ card, and says, "Oh, I know that he will rise on the last day ... but that doesn't help me here, right now. I want him alive. And you weren't here. Jesus, if you'd a been here, my brother would not have died." Do you hear the anger?

Jesus then shares some words. It isn't a cute story about when he and Lazarus went fishing one day. It wasn't flowery words about how everyone loved Lazarus. He didn't mention what a good

Christian Lazarus was nor did he give Martha one of those, "There, there. It'll be okay." He said the only thing to say at a funeral. "I am the resurrection and the life. Anyone who believes in me will live, even after dying" (John 11:25, NLT). Then came the punch line, "Do you believe this, Martha?" (John 11:26, NLT).

"I am the resurrection and the life." Those are the words that need to be said at a funeral. Those are the words that need to be heard on All Saints because they are the final word. The last remaining question is, "Do you believe this?"

There are so many other words and voices vying for our attention at a funeral. The Hallmark™ card wants to summarize our grief in a two-line limerick. The back of the mortuary card tells us the person is not gone but somehow present in the sunrise and the morning breeze. Our neighbor consults the stars, the spiritualist wants to meditate, the palm reader wants to look at your hand, and the atheist has nothing to say. People look and listen in all sorts of places, desperate to hear some answers and so they consult New Age to witchcraft to aroma therapy to a stiff drink. What do you say at a funeral?

The answer is: nothing. At least nothing from us. This is a time for God's word to be heard. Listen to the power and authority and hope and faith that Paul uses to describe the sure and certain hope that is ours in Jesus.

> *I pray that your hearts will be flooded with light so that you can understand the wonderful future he has promised to those he called. I want you to realize what a rich and glorious inheritance he has given to his people. I pray that you will begin to understand the incredible greatness of his power for us who believe in him....*
> — Ephesians 1:18-19

Our voice is the last thing that needs to be heard at a funeral. Our voice cannot lift the fog. Our voice cannot restore the hope. Our voice cannot raise the dead. There is only one voice that can do all of that. The voice that told his followers not just to hear his words but to follow him. The voice that did not correct Thomas when he cried out, "My Lord and my God." The voice who said if you have seen me, you have seen God. The voice that made it clear that he gave his life for the forgiveness of sins. The voice that says even through tears, "I am the resurrection and the life; he who believes in me, though he die, yet shall he live" (John 11:25 RSV).

That voice alone has the final word particularly on All Saints when we remember those who have died when each one of us feels this pain, this emptiness, this sadness, and even this anger and guilt from missing that person. Particularly on this day, more than any other day, we need to sift through all the noise, all the voices, all the garbage, and long to hear that one voice of truth and authority that alone can raise the dead.

What is that final word? What is that hope to which we've been called? That word is grace. Jesus came not to make bad people good through his example of purity but to make dead people live through his cross of forgiveness.

We did go through with Jason's funeral — the brother who made all those bad choices, burned bridges, and hurt feelings. We had his funeral. But we didn't list his Eagle Scout badge or mention the little old ladies he helped across the street or recall his generous heart and his deep love, because frankly, it wasn't true. Everyone in that room knew it wasn't true. No one dared say that they wished God would judge him on all the good that he did, because there wasn't much.

On that day, there was only one voice to be heard. The voice that spoke at Jason's funeral was the same that spoke at Lazarus' funeral and the same that spoke through the hope found in Paul's words to the Ephesians. It will be the same voice, the only voice that needs to be heard at your funeral. The voice of forgiveness. The only voice that can raise the dead. The voice of Jesus.

The family needed to hear forgiveness. All those hurt feelings and broken promises and bad choices — it was time to let them go. With death taking away the possibility of reconciling with Jason, they had a choice. They could harbor resentment and let it eat at their heart, or they could hear the voice of forgiveness and let it go.

Jason needed forgiveness. He was not a saint, but Jesus did not come for the saints. He came for the sick, the outcast, and the sinner. Jesus came for the likes of Jason because the playing field is level before the holy throne of God — knee level. We all approach not with a resume of good works, kind acts, and strong intentions but on our knees by faith right next to Jason.

There is only one voice I want to hear at my funeral. It is not a family member reciting how much we loved each other. It's not a friend retelling an embarrassing story about me. It's not a pastor reciting my accomplishments. There is only one voice, one final word that I want spoken at my funeral — the sure and certain hope that comes through the forgiveness of sins.

I pray that your hearts will be flooded with light so that you can understand the wonderful future he has promised to those he called. I want you to realize what a rich and glorious inheritance he has given to his people. I pray that you will begin to understand the incredible greatness of his power for us who believe in him. Amen.

**Proper 26
Pentecost 24
Ordinary Time 31
2 Thessalonians 1:1-4, 11-12**

Worthy Of Your Call

> *... we always pray for you, that our God may make you worthy of his call....*
> — 2 Thessalonians 1:11 (RSV)

Worthy of your call. That is Paul's prayer for the Thessalonians; that they would be worthy of God's call (1:11). It is one thing to have low expectations, something that would take little effort to achieve. But in chapter 1 of 2 Thessalonians, we have a sense that God has larger aspirations for these young Christians — and so does Paul. You have a sense that through all the persecution and affliction that they have suffered (1:4), Paul envisions a God-sized dream for them.

What are your God-sized dreams? These are the dreams that you cannot achieve alone with just more education, more hours, more determination, and more contacts. These are dreams that only God can achieve by working through the likes of you, a flawed, cracked vessel. These are dreams that have nothing to do with your quick wit and winning smile. It may be a dream to grow a church that reaches thousands. It may be a program that will help transform a neighborhood. It may even be dreams of running for public office and truly serving the people. If all obstacles were taken away, what are your God-sized dreams?

Fulfilling that God-sized dream would be "worthy of your call."

What happens when the path leading to that dream is marked with the kind of persecution, affliction, and suffering these people from Thessalonica have suffered? What happens when what seemed to be the right path is suddenly blocked with obstacles beyond your control? How do you prove to be worthy of your call when your life is no longer energized by God-sized dreams but rather with nightmares that plunge you further in the pit?

I want to share with you a powerful testimony I heard Phil Vischer give while speaking at a conference at Willow Creek in Chicago. Have you heard of Phil Vischer? I had not, at least by name. But I certainly knew about his product. He is the creator of *VeggieTales*. Have you heard of *VeggieTales*? If you haven't, *VeggieTales* are animated, short videos for children featuring limbless vegetables acting out Bible stories and moral truths. When you put it that way, it doesn't sound very impressive, does it? However, consider this:

- *VeggieTales* has sold 40 million videos.
- In 1999 and 2000, *VeggieTales* outsold Barney, Scooby Doo, and Pokémon combined.
- Those same years, CNN announced that *VeggieTales* was listed in the top ten videos watched on college campuses.
- In 2000, Vischer was named as one of the top ten religious leaders in America with write ups in *Newsweek*, *Time*, and *People* magazines.

VeggieTales was an incredible, nearly overnight success story headed up a guy who, as he describes himself, was kicked out of Bible college after three semesters for failing chapel. He left school to pursue his God-sized dream. This was a man of faith who wanted to make a deep impact for the kingdom, not just sell videos and retire early in southern Florida. He caught the attention of Disney who surrounded him with a staff of over 200 people who whispered around the water cooler, "Phil Vischer is the next Walt Disney." Unbelievable!

In a sense, this was like the young church in Thessalonica. They had heard the gospel from Paul. He filled them with God-sized dreams coupled with the power of the Holy Spirit. They were on fire for their faith, ready to move mountains and transform the world, until persecution knocked the wind out of them.

In the case of Vischer, it was a former distributor who took him to court. Vischer knew that he was in the right but it doesn't matter when you are presented with a lawsuit. You go to court, you spend lots of money on lawyers, and in the end you are at the mercy of the court who decided against Vischer and gave the distributor everything they asked for ... and much more. Vischer had to close down the studio, lay off the staff, and sell *VeggieTales* in order to pay off the enormous debt. As quickly as this God-sized dream had grown, it disappeared. For Vischer, *VeggieTales* was finished.

How can you be worthy of your call with affliction like that?

Stunned, Vischer wondered, "How could you, God? How could you give me this incredible gift and then sit back and do nothing as I watched it die? How could you? How could you promise me this dream, deliver this dream, and then pop this dream?"

After a long time in prayer and reading his Bible, Vischer was drawn to Genesis 22 — Abraham's sacrifice of Isaac. Remember how Abraham was given a promise that his descendants would be more numerous than grains of sand? They would outnumber the stars. Sure, he had to wait a long time for the dream to actualize — 25 years of waiting. But now, the God-sized dream came true with Isaac. The God-sized dreams of descendants numbering more than grains of sands and stars in the sky could begin. Now Abraham could be worthy of his call.

Except, in Genesis 22, God says to Abraham, "Take your son, your only son, the one whom you love (and just so there is no misunderstanding), the one named Isaac and sacrifice him to me." God did not want Isaac's death. It was a test with only one question. "What is more important to you — the dream or God?" As Abraham raised his knife to Isaac, God knew that Abraham was willing to surrender and let go of everything, even his God-sized dream. He was willing to put it all on the altar and watch it die — everything, except for knowing and trusting God.

Through that experience of Abraham, Phil Vischer realized that he had confused doing the work of God with knowing God. His goal was to make a great impact, to reach more people, to do more wonderful things for God. All great and wonderful things. However, it was not to know God. Phil understood what had happened with *VeggieTales* as God was asking him to sacrifice his dream on the altar for the sake of keeping his eyes on Jesus. He had gotten ahead of God. He was asking God to catch up to him and bless what he had done. Bottom line: He had taken his eyes off Jesus.

Then Vischer asked a question to the congregation, "What do you dream that you can do for God? Expand your ministry? Increase membership? Impact more people? Build a bigger church? What do you dream that you can do for God?"

It is not a question to be taken lightly or answered flippantly. For a deeper affect, Vischer let the question hang in the air for several minutes until he concluded, "When you are ready to put that dream on the altar and kill it for the sake of knowing God, then you are ready."

Then you are ready. Or, in Paul's words, then you are worthy of your call.

Make no doubt here. Paul is not encouraging the Thessalonians to continue in their food pantry ministry. Paul is not advising them on how to plant another church. Paul is not asking them for more money. For Paul, to be worthy of your call is found in 1:3-4.

> ... *your faith is growing abundantly, and the love of everyone of you for one another is increasing. Therefore we ourselves boast of you among the churches of God for your steadfastness and faith during all your persecutions and the afflictions that you are enduring.*
> — 2 Thessalonians 1:3-4

To be worthy of your call is to keep your eyes fixed on Jesus. Everything else needs to be put on the altar and, at a moment's notice, be plunged with a knife. For the first commandment is clear; you shall have no other gods before me. This includes even your God-sized dreams. Amen.

**Proper 27
Pentecost 25
Ordinary Time 32
2 Thessalonians 2:1-5, 13-17**

Sarah

*Don't be so easily shaken or alarmed by those who say
that the day of the Lord has already begun.*
— 2 Thessalonians 2:2 (NLT)

Max Lucado, in his book, *In the Eye of the Storm*, writes about a woman named Sarah who was rich.[1] Really rich! She inherited twenty million dollars plus had an additional income of $1,000 a day. That's a lot of money today. But in the late 1800s when Sarah lived, it was downright staggering.

You can imagine that she was well-known, having come from the elite, upper crust of the New England coast. Well-known and powerful. Her name and money opened doors closed to most of us. Colleges wanted her scholarships. Politicians wanted her support. Organizations wanted her donations.

Did I mention that she was rich? And powerful? And well-known? She was also miserable. Her only daughter died when she was five weeks old and her husband died shortly afterward, following their daughter to the grave. This left Sarah alone with her money, her memories, her misery, and enough guilt to max out even *her* credit cards.

It was primarily this last burden of her guilt that made her leave the luxury of her mansion in Connecticut and ride the train until its very last whistle stop in San Jose, California. It's amazing the distance we will travel to escape the reminders, silence the voices, and avoid the reality. She did escape — right into a prison of her own making.

She bought an eight-room farmhouse and 160 acres of land. She hired sixteen carpenters and put them to work — for 38 years. Every day. Twenty-four hours. She hired them to build, what? A mansion or was it a castle? Better yet, it was more like a prison.

Sarah oversaw the entire project all the way down to the eerie, macabre details like thirteen panes on each window, thirteen panels on each wall, thirteen hooks in each closet, and thirteen globes in each chandelier.

The floor plan was just as creepy. There were corridors snaking around the complex, some going nowhere. One door opened to a blank wall, another to a fifty-foot drop. One set of stairs led to a ceiling that had no door. Trapdoors, secret passageways, tunnels — think of the latest Stephen King horror movie and you get the picture.

The construction didn't end until Sarah finally died. In those 38 years, the estate sprawled over six acres with six kitchens, thirteen bathrooms, forty stairways, 47 fireplaces, 52 skylights, 467 inside doors, 10,000 windows, 160 rooms, and a bell tower.

Why? Why would you build such a place? Because you could afford it? That's too easy. There had to be something more to it than extravagance or opulence. Those acquainted with her said it was because she had so many visitors ... each night.

Legend has it that every evening at midnight a servant would pass through the secret labyrinth of tunnels to the bell tower. He would then ring the bell to summon the ghosts who would convene nightly in the blue room with Sarah. Together, they would linger until 2 a.m. when the bell would ring again. The spirits would return to their graves, and Sarah would return to her room.

Who were these spirits that haunted the mansion and would not let Sarah sleep? The legend says that they are all the Indians and soldiers and cowboys killed on the US frontier. Men, women, and children who were killed by bullets from the most popular and effective rifle and killing machine known in America — The Winchester. The same thing that brought death to these people brought millions of dollars to Sarah ... Sarah Winchester.

And now, as Paul Harvey would say, you know the rest of the story.

Sarah spent the last 38 years of her life trapped in a castle of memories, providing a home for the restless dead, and learning how to cope with her guilt ... according to legend, at least.

You don't have to build a Winchester mansion to deal with unresolved guilt or fear of the future. I suppose we all figure out different ways, more creative ways, less expensive ways to assuage a heart that just can't seem forget or ignore a page from our past or a lie in our present or the unknown of the future.

Some of us, like Sarah, are doomed to wander the halls and entertain those poltergeists in the dead of the night when they rise to haunt us, robbing us of sleep, and preventing peace.

Maybe you know a Sarah? Maybe Sarah's story is your story. Different portfolio, different floor plan, but same insatiable quest for forgiveness and resolution.

The answers to guilt's questions are not found in a new house. The answers are not found in a distracted life. The answers are not found in simply learning how to live with the restlessness. The answers are found in the one who has the power to forgive and forget. The answers are found in the one who promises to return to those who await him and give what they have waited a lifetime to hear.

Scholars say that 2 Thessalonians was written shortly after 1 Thessalonians as a way for Paul to clarify the widespread misunderstanding of Paul's teachings concerning the return of Jesus. Many who read the first letter thought that the end time had already begun. Judging from the content of 2 Thessalonians, many had quit work, fallen into despair, and lived with a constant fear.

> *And now, brothers and sisters, let us tell you about the coming again of our Lord Jesus Christ and how we will be gathered together to meet him. Please don't be so easily shaken and troubled by those who say that the day of the Lord has already begun.*
> — 2 Thessalonians 2:1-2 (NLT)

Paul wrote this follow-up letter to reprimand them sharply, to remind them of the true teaching, and to encourage them to live lives that would prepare them for Jesus' return. It is not a letter filled with fear and horrible images of damnation. Instead, Paul reminds them of the hope that is theirs to come.

> *As for us, we always thank God for you, dear brothers and sisters loved by the Lord. We are thankful that God chose you to be among the first to experience salvation, a salvation that came through the Spirit who makes you holy and by your belief in the truth.*
> — 2 Thessalonians 2:13 (NLT)

Paul needs to remind these young Christians who have either fallen into despair or tremble with fear about Jesus' authority to forgive sins. To have the power to forgive a person's sins is reserved only for the one who has the power, who has the authority, who sits on the right side of God as judge over the living and the dead and who promised to return one day for the cleansing of those who believe in him.

That's what the Son of Man does. That's what he came to do. That's what he has the power to perform. He forgives and then goes one step further. He forgets. He erases the board, shreds the evidence, destroys the chip, and deletes the screen. For all the things that the Son of Man promises to do for us, the one thing that he refuses to do is to remember.

> *... as far as the east is from the west, so far he removes our transgressions from us.* — Psalm 103:12

> *Even if you are stained as red as crimson, I can make you white as wool.* — Isaiah 1:18 (NLT)

> *I will be their God, and they shall be my people ... and I will remember their sins no more.*
> — Hebrews 8:10, 12

Do you believe that?

Jesus gives us a double promise; to forgive and forget. But we don't, do we? Not as easily, anyway. We have a good memory.

We are more like Sarah who entertains the ghosts of our past that still linger, robbing us of sleep and peace. What these demons that go bump in the night are doing, really, is trying to get you to forget whose you are. They are giving your spiritual journey a limp from some irritable stone in your sandal. They fill us with doubts whether or not God could actually do what he promises — forgive and forget. That's the gift that Jesus, the Son of Man, judge of the world gives to us — a terrible memory. He doesn't keep record of those past sins on his clipboard to check it next time you get on your knees and say you're sorry. Instead, his gift is a grace filled, mercy driven, terrible memory so you don't drive yourself crazy hanging out with the ghosts of the past.

You don't have to learn to live with your past and cope with your guilt like Sarah Winchester. You don't have to tremble and be shaken like those young Thessalonians. Jesus offers a cure.

My wife and I recently saw *A Beautiful Mind*. It has been a long time since a movie has made such an impact on me. It's about a lot of things — friendship, marriage, commitment, and love. It is also about mental illness. The movie suggests what I have always thought was most often the case with mental illness. That is, most people suffering from mental illness are not "cured" like some physical diseases through treatment, drugs, or surgery. Most often those with mental illness learn how to cope or live with or even ignore their illness — but it is still always there. Those with depression, anxiety, or, as in the case of this movie, schizophrenia, it doesn't actually go away but you learn how to deal with it, learn how to live with it, even learn how to ignore it. This movie depicts mental illness more like a bad back or diabetes or alcoholism. It never goes away but you learn ways to cope with it.

That might work with diabetes or depression. We might have wonderful drugs to mask the problems of anxiety or support groups to deal with addiction or exercises to ease lower back trouble. But when it comes to my guilt, I don't want a drug or a coping mechanism. I don't want to have to learn how to live with unresolved guilt, or cope with, live, or figure out how to ignore it. When it comes to sins, I'm not looking for a distraction or a class on how to live with it. There are too many Sarahs who are plagued with spirits of their past who rise when the sun goes down to make us doubt the very words of Jesus. I'm looking for someone who can bring a cure, wipe away all traces of it. I'm looking for a savior that Paul describes — one who forgives and forgets.

Maybe that is why when others refer to Jesus, they use Lord, Messiah, or Christ, and he is. But when Jesus refers to himself, by far the most common title he uses is Son of Man — the one who has the power and authority and might to heal us at our deepest level; at the level of our guilt with the power of his word, "Not guilty, for Jesus' sake."

Now you know the rest of the story. Amen.

---

1. Max Lucado, *In The Eye of the Storm* (Nashville: Thomas Nelson, 2001), p. 191.

**Proper 28
Pentecost 26
Ordinary Time 33
2 Thessalonians 3:6-13**

No Work, No Food!

Whoever does not work should not eat!
— 2 Thessalonians 3:10 (NLT)

Wow! Kind of takes your breath away, doesn't it? Not a lot of ambiguity in that rule. "You don't work, you don't eat." For a religion based on grace, it seems a bit unyielding.

You would expect that rule in our ever-productive society. After all, it seems that our worth is determined by how much we can produce. Therefore, we judge others on how much (or how little) they are contributing. But is this really the way we ought to proceed in our faith? Should productivity be the measure by which we decide whether or not a person is deserving of food?

I grew up in a family that could not stand idle time. They originated the saying, "Don't just sit there — do something!" It was most apparent when one of us got the flu. When one of us got sick, we were handed a sleeve of saltine crackers and a liter of Seven-Up® and sent to our rooms until we could become a productive member of society once again! (Okay, that is a bit of an exaggeration but you get the point. Thankfully, they still fed us during bed rest even if we did not work.) I understand a high work ethic.

When I read these strong words from Paul in 2 Thessalonians, I contrast it to the parable told by Jesus in Matthew 20:1-15 where day laborers went into the marketplace at dawn and the owners of the vineyards would go and hire as many workers as they needed. The going wage for one day of work was one denarius.

However, in the parable, one owner miscalculated the number of workers he needed. He returned to the marketplace four times: 9 a.m., noon, 3 p.m., and again at 5 p.m. just one hour before the whistle blew. Those who were hired at 9 a.m. expected the one denarius as payment. However, for those hired later in the day, all the owner said was, "I will pay you whatever is right." No contract. Just a promise.

Of course, you know how the story ends. They all line up after work for their paychecks. Beginning with the 5 p.m. workers, the owner pays everyone the same amount — one denarius. When those who were hired at the crack of dawn made it to the front of the line, they expected something more in their paychecks, but were disappointed to find out that their full-day work amounted to the same paycheck as those Johnny-come-latelys who only worked for one hour.

Jesus' parable reminds us that in the kingdom of God, all are seen as equals. From those who were baptized as infants to the thief on the cross who made it through the gates at the eleventh hour, all are treated equally. Does that mean that we can sleep in late, grab a late brunch with a Belgian waffle topped with whipped cream and fresh strawberries, catch the afternoon show of *Oprah*, and then around 5 p.m. show up for an hour of work?

You can hear from those who bore the heat of the full day cry out, "Unfair!" You can't give everyone the same pay. You can't give everyone the same grade. The whole class cannot be valedictorians. The entire team cannot be the captain. The entire business cannot be owners. Life is full of comparisons, some are higher, some are lower. It just goes against everything we do and believe to make all the workers equal. They grumble, "He made the ones who worked only for a few hours equal to those who bore the burden of the entire day."

Here is where the confusion lies — equality.

In the parable, Jesus is talking about our justification. Between the long time believer and the eleventh-hour-thief-on-the-cross, there is no distinction. There is no gradation in heaven. There is nothing extra in your paycheck when you pass through the pearly gates at the end of the day. Jesus is talking about how we are saved.

In the end, it doesn't matter if we believed our whole lives or had a deathbed conversion. We are all beggars in need of God's grace. None is deserving of more. Ironically, Jesus puts the gospel in the words of the grumblers when they say, "He made the ones who worked for only a few hours equal to those who bore the burden of the entire day." Exactly! That is the grace found in the kingdom of God.

But in 2 Thessalonians, Paul is talking about how we ought to live. In theological jargon, Jesus spoke about justification and Paul spoke about sanctification. Just like we cannot read Paul to defend works righteousness, we cannot read Jesus to defend laziness.

However, underlining both of their teachings is the same point — entitlement. Once we cross over that line from humility and gratitude to entitlement and demands, we miss seeing the surprise of the gospel at work in our lives.

To the longtime believer who approaches the throne of heaven with a laundry list of accomplishments from regular worship attendance to generous donations to volunteering at the soup kitchen, they are in for a surprise to find that many will cry out, "Lord, Lord" but he will not know them. Tradition has it that on his deathbed, after a lifetime of faithful service, Luther continued to preach grace by saying, "We are all beggars. This is most certainly true."

No one ought to have the arrogance of entitlement coming before the throne of God, demanding that to get exactly what you deserve — nothing more or nothing less. Such a demand for justice would only bring with it exactly that — damnation, judgment, and death. What Jesus taught in Matthew 20 was that entitlement does not enter into our ability to stand before God's throne.

Neither does entitlement factor into Paul's teaching in 2 Thessalonians.

Our church like many other congregations volunteers often at the local soup kitchen or homeless shelter. We don't turn away people due to gender or race or religion. We don't even turn away people because of a sense of entitlement. But there are certainly those guests who come with gratitude in their heart, thankful for what can be provided. And there are others who come with a sense of entitlement, demanding more than we have and ungrateful for what we can offer. We haven't come to the point of enforcing Paul's command, but we certainly understand Paul's point — if you don't work, you don't eat.

It comes down to entitlement. God does not have to forgive our sins, grant us mercy, and receive us into the kingdom. None of us are entitled. He does so out of love. In the same way, it is difficult to imagine that same entitlement thinking being appropriate at the soup kitchen or homeless shelter.

Rudyard Kipling, author of the *Jungle Book*, at the height of his career received large payments for even the shortest articles. Some struggling literature majors in England resented his success. After reading a report that Kipling had received a large sum for a short story, these students divided up the payment by the number of words in the essay and calculated that Kipling was paid fifty cents per word. With dripping sarcasm, the students mailed Kipling fifty cents and asked him to give them his best word. In a brief time, the students receive a letter from the author with only one word, "Thanks."

It is with such humility and gratitude that we approach both the throne of God as well as receive help from others — thanks. Amen.

Christ The King
Proper 29
Colossians 1:11-20

This Is A King?

He is the image of the invisible God, the firstborn of all creation; for in him all things in heaven and on earth were created ... in him all the fullness of God was pleased to dwell... — Colossians 1:15-16, 19

I grew up during all those *Godfather* movies, and I never saw a single one. I don't know why. I was busy. It was a three-hour movie. I had to study. So when I heard jokes about a horse's head or making an offer that he couldn't refuse, I didn't get it. The same is true today, right? There are those who have not watched or read a single *Harry Potter* story or a single *Star Wars* movie. When they hear, "The Force be with you," some only think, "And also with you." They don't get it. That's true with many things. There are those who have never been on a golf course, never went sailing, and never had children. Their understanding of these things is limited.

There are even those who haven't heard much about Jesus except how to curse using his name. They've never cracked open a Bible. They've never darkened the door of a church. They've never attended Sunday school. Now, put yourself into their world and you hear that this Jesus

He is the image of the invisible God, the firstborn of all creation; for in him all things in heaven and on earth were created ... in him all the fullness of God was pleased to dwell... — Colossians 1:15-16, 19

You would expect someone like Jesus to stand out. You would expect someone like this to have words of wisdom. You would expect someone in whom the fullness of God dwelt to take your breath away. What you don't expect is the Jesus of the New Testament who says ...

> *Fortunate are those who are poor, Lucky are those who are hungry, Blessed are those who weep. If you are being persecuted, abused, beaten — rejoice.*
> — Matthew 5:3, 6, 11 (paraphrased)

> *Don't hate your enemies, love them. Do good things for them. If they hit you on one cheek, turn and let them strike you on the other. If they demand your coat, give them your shirt also.*
> — Matthew 5:40, 43-44

> *Also, you know that it is wrong to murder, but I tell you that even if you think angry thoughts about someone it is the same as murder. And you know that you should not commit adultery. But I tell you even looking at another person and having lustful fantasies, you are as guilty as the one who crawls into bed with him or her.*
> — Matthew 5:21, 27-28 (paraphrased)

Can you hear these words for the first time? Remember, you don't know that these words are from Jesus. You have heard nothing about the Sermon on the Mount. Lucky are the poor. Rejoice that you are beaten. Love your enemies. You think there's nothing wrong with cursing someone under your breath? You think there's no harm in just looking? Think again, you murderer. Reconsider, you adulterer. Now, what is your reaction? Honestly? It's got to be one of four.

First, *that's just stupid!* Philip Yancey in his book, *The Jesus I Never Knew*, quotes a professor at Texas A&M who had her English comp class read these words from the Beatitudes from Jesus and asked them to write an essay. She expected them to have some basic biblical knowledge but soon found out they had very little. She grew up in a church with a picture of Jesus teaching these words on a small mountain overseeing a green hillside surrounded by eager pink children.

She never heard these words with disgust or anger. But that is what her students wrote:

> The stuff the churches preach is extremely strict and allows for almost no fun without thinking it is a sin or not.
>
> The things asked in this sermon are absurd. To look at a woman is adultery. That is the most extreme, stupid, unhuman statement that I have ever heard.
>
> There is an old saying that you shouldn't believe everything you read and it applies in this case.

It never occurred to this professor that someone might call Jesus stupid. Yet what she heard from her students was a pure, unfiltered reaction to the words of Jesus that have not been spiritualized by the church. These words are offensive and when they were first uttered by Jesus, he didn't just puzzle the people, he infuriated them.

Second, *it isn't that nice!* It means you have no intention of taking it to heart. Jesus was just throwing out Hallmark™ card platitudes to the poor people, "God bless you." To those whose faces were wet with tears, Jesus comforted them, "Count your blessings." But we don't really believe it, do we?

Philip Yancey wrote that he and about a dozen evangelicals were invited to breakfast with President Clinton. Clinton was low in the polls with conservative Christians, and he wanted to hear from them. Each guest was given five minutes. What should he say? Yancey thought he should say what Jesus would have said:

> Mr. President, first I want to advise you to stop worrying so much about the economy and jobs. A lower Gross National Product is actually good for the country because the more poor we have in America, the more blessed we are.
>
> And don't worry about health care. You see, Mr. President, the more people who weep and mourn, the more fortunate that we are.

> *And I know that you have heard from the "Religious Right" about prayer taken out of schools and protesters against abortion being arrested. Relax, sir. More government oppression actually gives Christians an opportunity to be persecuted and we want to thank you for those expanded opportunities.*

He didn't share those words with the president. Why? Because we really don't believe it. No one is striving to be more poor, more hungry, or more abused. This is America! Happy are the strong, the rich, the healthy, and the confident.

Even the church thinks this way. The theologian, Soren Kierkegaard, once attended a large cathedral in Europe that took decades to build and cost millions of dollars. The priest stood before an ivory altar in his silver threaded chasuble, lifted up the gold chalice of fine wine and read, "Blessed are the poor, blessed are the hungry ..." and Kierkegaard looked around and realized no one laughed. If they took Jesus' words seriously, there should be laughter because even the church isn't living it. Blessed are the poor? Isn't that nice? Bless his heart.

There is a third response from those who hear these words and think, *if that is what Jesus said, then I'll do it*. Let me tell you about Linda. Linda's not right. Linda's from New York where she had a home and a job and family. She said that God put it on her heart to leave it all and do ministry in Romania. She contacted "Smiles," an organization in Great Britain that works with the poor of Romania and told them of her intentions. The director, Kevin Hoy, said, "That's fine but have you been to Romania before?"

"No," she replied.

"Do you think you should come once before you quit your job and sell everything?"

She did, but only to appease the director. Her mind was made up. If Jesus called us to serve the poor, then Linda needed to roll up her sleeves and begin the work.

In Romania, Linda lives alone and raises pigs and chickens for food that are slaughtered for the poor. She's a city girl who spends her time cleaning out the pig sty. She gets up about 5 a.m. to go out and water the many acres of cucumbers, tomatoes, corn, and peppers while singing, "How Great Thou Art." She says that the plants think that she is singing about them and they like it.

She gets no salary. She has to raise all of her living expenses; nothing is provided for her. Her one luxury is a bath twice a week. For the past couple of years, I've brought Linda a jar of peanut butter when I travel with a missionary team to Romania. From her reaction, you would think it was filet and lobster.

I look at Linda, I hear her love for the pigs and the vegetables and how they will feed the hungry children we work with there. I hear her joy about living with the poor of Romania. I hear her sacrifice of what she has given up to serve God. And I think, she's not right. Even if I were single and had few responsibilities, I still wouldn't do that. Linda's not right. But in my heart, I know Linda is right, more right with God than I am.

Which brings me to the fourth response to these strange words of Jesus. *How is it that Jesus made the law impossible for anyone to follow and then demands us to keep it?* If I am angry with someone, I'm a murderer? If I have a lustful thought, I'm an adulterer? Give away all that I have to the poor? If my hand causes me to sin, cut it off? Do not worry about tomorrow? What am I to do? Cash out my IRA and scatter it among the panhandlers? Cancel my insurance and trust God? Throw out my television and cancel the newspaper and magazines with the ads that tempt me to buy more?

If these words of Jesus are not stupid, if they are not some Hallmark™ card platitude (isn't that nice), if they are true then the bar is too high for me to reach. If these words are true, they drop me to my knees and reveal to me just how far short I fall of Jesus. Now what?

It is right there, at that fourth response, dropped to our knees that we grasp the very heart of Jesus' message on this Christ The King Sunday. You misunderstand this and you misunderstand the very core of Jesus' teachings. You miss this and you miss who he really is.

> *He is the image of the invisible God, the firstborn of all creation; for in him all things in heaven and on earth*

> *were created ... In him all the fullness of God was pleased to dwell...*   — Colossians 1:15-16, 19

These words of Jesus are not so much telling us what we should be like but what God is like. Even Linda, who is trying to be obedient to these words of Jesus, knows how far short she falls from the glory of God. She's been dropped to her knees. She knows that the chasm that separates her from God is huge and that at the last trumpet sound, when Christ the King will stand upon the earth, we all will stand on level ground before the throne of God — murderers, temper-throwers, adulterers, lusters, thieves, coveters. We are all desperate and in need of a king who is first a Savior.

Jesus the king came to make self-absorbed, guilt-driven, dead people alive with the only words that make a difference, the only words that will drop you to your knees, the only words that matter when he returns — "Your sins are forgiven for Jesus' sake."

That's not crazy talk. That's not Hallmark™. That is the very heart of Jesus' promise to return as King of kings and Lord of lords; so that you might know, believe, confess, and walk daily in the shadow of the cross and in the grace of God. Amen.

**Thanksgiving Day
Philippians 4:4-9**

A New Resolve

"Stand firm in the Lord" (Philippians 4:1).

Last summer, my children rode a flight simulator. Basically, they strap you into a box in front of a screen and shake it upside down. It is supposed to feel more like flying an airplane than a Disney ride. They also had a camera on the people inside the simulator so that those waiting outside can see what was going on inside the cockpit. When my daughter had the controls, the plane was level, missed the trees, and landed smoothly. When my son took over the controls, the box spun with barrel rolls, shot straight up, and then dove nose first into a spectacular crash landing.

All fun and games but not to a real pilot. They spend hours in that little box not for amusement but to train themselves and to prepare for worst-case scenarios so that when lightning does hit or an engine goes out or a landing gear is stuck in real life, they will know what to do. Without that training and foundation, they would be lost.

Can you imagine going into battle without the foundation of basic training? Can you imagine going into a highly technical computer job without some basic training in computers? Can you imagine going through job loss, divorce, or death without the foundation of new hope?

The point is, you need some basic training, some foundation, before going into a cockpit, battle, or surgery. Paul uses that same logic when he talks about life. To introduce our lesson in Philippians 4:4-9, Paul begins in 4:1 with the imperative, "Stand firm in the Lord." The imagery that Paul is using with this phrase is that of a guard or a sentry who, with weapon in hand, stands firm. He is guarding something or someone. He makes sure that nothing will get through him, not on his watch.

Paul is telling us to do the same thing. Stand firm. Do not be caught off guard. As I look at 4:4-9, the word that comes to mind is "resolve." Stand firm with resolve. The time for the pilot to figure out how to land a plane with a blown engine is not mid-air. The time for a married couple to figure out how to fight fairly is not in the middle of the argument. The time for the young adult to figure out their sexuality is not in the moment of passion. Paul is saying that the time for the Christian to decide how to respond in crisis is not when you are overcome by pain, grief, and doubt. Resolve right now how you will act, respond, and speak while you are still in the simulator. To be sure, real life is far more intense and unpredictable than a simulator but start building that foundation now.

Paul knew what he wrote about. Remember, Paul wrote this letter while beaten and imprisoned in Rome, awaiting his execution. Yet he wrote, "Rejoice in the Lord always" (v. 4). How can Paul write that? Because long before he was thrown into prison, Paul decided how he would respond. He resolved in his own mind how to stand firm, how to guard his heart and mind. And now he shares three very specific things for us to guard.

First, *guard your relationship with God*. Paul begins by writing, "Do not worry about anything" (v. 6). Isn't that crazy? That must be the most difficult command to obey. If someone were to come to me saying that he lost his job, was going through bankruptcy, his wife was leaving him, his children were strung out on drugs, and now he wants to end it all, could you imagine simply saying, "Don't worry about anything"? That would be crazy. So how does Paul get away with it? Because it is not an emotion that Paul is commanding. It's a relationship with God. When that breaks down, worry increases because most worry is not trusting God. Most worry is unnecessary and destructive. A recent study discovered that:

- 40% of our worries never happen,
- 30% of our worries concern the past,

- 12% of our worries are needless about health,
- 10% of our worries are insignificant and petty, and
- 8% of our worries are legitimate, appropriate worries.

Even Jesus said in Matthew 6 not to worry about tomorrow because tomorrow will have its own worries. Let the day's own worries be sufficient for the day. So there are some things to worry about but they are few. The rest is highly destructive and reveals a lack of trust in God.

What's the answer? One church sign read, "Why pray when you can worry and take tranquilizers?" Paul would disagree. He says, "Don't panic, pray. Be a person of prayer." "In everything by prayer and supplication with thanksgiving let your requests be made known to God" (v. 6b).

Second, *guard your thoughts.* "Finally, beloved, whatever is true, whatever is honorable, whatever is just, whatever is pure, whatever is pleasing, whatever is commendable, if there is any excellence and if there is anything worthy of praise, think about these things" (v. 8). Guard your thoughts.

We become what we think. Did you know that? Proverbs 23:7 says, "As a man thinks in his heart, so is he." I read one quote that put it well: "Sow a thought, reap an action. Sow an action, reap a habit. Sow a habit, reap a character. Sow a character, reap a destiny." We become what we think. Therefore, Paul puts out eight filters for us to determine whether or not this guard, this sentry, is in our minds and hearts. Is it true, honorable, just, pure, and so on? Because there is a lot of stuff out there that is not.

We pay $10 a month for cable. Basic cable. It's not much, as my kids keep reminding me. I would like to get ESPN. I would like to get Discovery. But I can't get those two without letting in a whole lot of garbage into my house that's not true, just, pure, pleasing, and so on. We argue about what movies to see because I don't want some images to be in my children's hearts and minds. I'm concerned at some sleepovers that it will be different elsewhere. When we download iTunes, we check out the lyrics.

This has always been an issue. Nothing has changed. Polluting the mind must have been an issue in Philippi. It certainly was for

Luther. He said, "You can't stop a bird from flying overhead but you can stop it from nesting in your hair."

The mind and heart will be filled with images and thoughts. Paul is saying if you want to stand firm and live with resolve before the crisis hits, then guard your thoughts. Ask yourself, "Is it true, pure, just, acceptable?"

Third, *guard your examples. Keep on doing the things that you have learned and received and heard and seen in me.* Is that arrogant? A little bit earlier, Paul said, "Join in imitating me. Let me be your example." Is that conceited? I don't think so. I think it is mentoring. Christian mentoring. We all need examples.

When I'm confronted with a tough theological question, I think, "WWLD" "What would Luther do?" He would stand firm on justification by faith alone. When I'm confronted with a tough pastoral issue, I think, "WWCD" what would Charlie do? (Charlie was my first senior pastor who taught me about the ministry.) When I'm trying to figure out how to handle a delicate issue with another person, I think "WWGD" what would Gretchen do? (She's my wife who is a whole lot nicer than I am!) Surround yourselves with the best examples.

Paul is a mature Christian. He is writing to baby Christians. He has seen a lot more, experienced a lot more. He can say, "Learn from me, follow me, listen to me," not with arrogance but with some wisdom gained over the years. We can do the same.

My most successful counseling sessions happen when I get out of the way. When I talk with someone in the middle of crisis who needs advice, I say, "I want you to talk to so and so." I give them the name of a person in the church who has gone through the same ordeal and lived to tell about it. They have learned for their experience and can say what Paul said, "learn from me, follow me, listen to me," not out of arrogance but out of experience.

Paul says, "Guard those examples. Surround yourselves with those examples. Learn from those examples." And then, let's be bold. Go one step further. Be that example — to others. Be that example. Because others are watching. It's been said that children learn what they live. Look up the poem "Children Learn What They Live" by Dorothy Law Nolte online.

Guard your relationship with God. Guard your thoughts. Guard your examples.

And then Paul makes a promise. If you do this, "the peace of God will guard your hearts and your minds." You deliberately, consciously, faithfully guard relationships, those thoughts and those examples and you will find that God's peace will place a sentry inside of you and guard your heart and mind when crisis hits.

When will that be? Unfortunately, none of us knows. There are times, however, in which my mind wanders and I think — how would I hold up if a September 11 attack hit my family? How would I hold up if a Hurricane Katrina hit my home? How would I hold up if that drunk driver took my wife? How would I hold up if it were my child in that hospital bed? I don't think any of us know for sure but this much is certain. There will come a day in which you will walk out of that simulator and into real life. That's not the time to figure it out. Paul's saying, "Now. Now is the time."

Guard your relationship with God. Guard those thoughts that enter in. Guard those examples so that when you leave this room, this simulator, and enter the real world, you can stand firm with a new resolve. Amen.

Lectionary Preaching After Pentecost

The following index will aid the user of this book in matching the correct Sunday with the appropriate text during Pentecost. All texts in this book are from the series for the Second Readings, Revised Common Lectionary. (Note that the ELCA division of Lutheranism is now following the Revised Common Lectionary.) The Lutheran designations indicate days comparable to Sundays on which Revised Common Lectionary Propers or Ordinary Time designations are used.

(Fixed dates do not pertain to Lutheran Lectionary)

Fixed Date Lectionaries *Revised Common (including ELCA)* *and Roman Catholic*	Lutheran Lectionary *Lutheran*
The Day Of Pentecost	The Day Of Pentecost
The Holy Trinity	The Holy Trinity
May 29-June 4 — Proper 4, Ordinary Time 9	Pentecost 2
June 5-11 — Proper 5, Ordinary Time 10	Pentecost 3
June 12-18 — Proper 6, Ordinary Time 11	Pentecost 4
June 19-25 — Proper 7, Ordinary Time 12	Pentecost 5
June 26-July 2 — Proper 8, Ordinary Time 13	Pentecost 6
July 3-9 — Proper 9, Ordinary Time 14	Pentecost 7
July 10-16 — Proper 10, Ordinary Time 15	Pentecost 8
July 17-23 — Proper 11, Ordinary Time 16	Pentecost 9
July 24-30 — Proper 12, Ordinary Time 17	Pentecost 10
July 31-Aug. 6 — Proper 13, Ordinary Time 18	Pentecost 11
Aug. 7-13 — Proper 14, Ordinary Time 19	Pentecost 12
Aug. 14-20 — Proper 15, Ordinary Time 20	Pentecost 13
Aug. 21-27 — Proper 16, Ordinary Time 21	Pentecost 14
Aug. 28-Sept. 3 — Proper 17, Ordinary Time 22	Pentecost 15
Sept. 4-10 — Proper 18, Ordinary Time 23	Pentecost 16
Sept. 11-17 — Proper 19, Ordinary Time 24	Pentecost 17
Sept. 18-24 — Proper 20, Ordinary Time 25	Pentecost 18

Sept. 25-Oct. 1 — Proper 21, Ordinary Time 26	Pentecost 19
Oct. 2-8 — Proper 22, Ordinary Time 27	Pentecost 20
Oct. 9-15 — Proper 23, Ordinary Time 28	Pentecost 21
Oct. 16-22 — Proper 24, Ordinary Time 29	Pentecost 22
Oct. 23-29 — Proper 25, Ordinary Time 30	Pentecost 23
Oct. 30-Nov. 5 — Proper 26, Ordinary Time 31	Pentecost 24
Nov. 6-12 — Proper 27, Ordinary Time 32	Pentecost 25
Nov. 13-19 — Proper 28, Ordinary Time 33	Pentecost 26
	Pentecost 27
Nov. 20-26 — Christ The King	Christ The King

Reformation Day (or last Sunday in October) is October 31 (Revised Common, Lutheran)

All Saints (or first Sunday in November) is November 1 (Revised Common, Lutheran, Roman Catholic)

US/Canadian Lectionary Comparison

The following index shows the correlation between the Sundays and special days of the church year as they are titled or labeled in the Revised Common Lectionary published by the Consultation On Common Texts and used in the United States (the reference used for this book) and the Sundays and special days of the church year as they are titled or labeled in the Revised Common Lectionary used in Canada.

Revised Common Lectionary	Canadian Revised Common Lectionary
Advent 1	Advent 1
Advent 2	Advent 2
Advent 3	Advent 3
Advent 4	Advent 4
Christmas Eve	Christmas Eve
The Nativity Of Our Lord/ Christmas Day	The Nativity Of Our Lord
Christmas 1	Christmas 1
January 1/New Year's Day	January 1/The Name Of Jesus
Christmas 2	Christmas 2
The Epiphany Of Our Lord	The Epiphany Of Our Lord
The Baptism Of Our Lord/ Epiphany 1	The Baptism Of Our Lord/ Proper 1
Epiphany 2/Ordinary Time 2	Epiphany 2/Proper 2
Epiphany 3/Ordinary Time 3	Epiphany 3/Proper 3
Epiphany 4/Ordinary Time 4	Epiphany 4/Proper 4
Epiphany 5/Ordinary Time 5	Epiphany 5/Proper 5
Epiphany 6/Ordinary Time 6	Epiphany 6/Proper 6
Epiphany 7/Ordinary Time 7	Epiphany 7/Proper 7
Epiphany 8/Ordinary Time 8	Epiphany 8/Proper 8
The Transfiguration Of Our Lord/ Last Sunday After Epiphany	The Transfiguration Of Our Lord/ Last Sunday After Epiphany
Ash Wednesday	Ash Wednesday
Lent 1	Lent 1
Lent 2	Lent 2
Lent 3	Lent 3
Lent 4	Lent 4
Lent 5	Lent 5
Passion/Palm Sunday	Passion/Palm Sunday
Maundy Thursday	Holy/Maundy Thursday
Good Friday	Good Friday

Easter Day	The Resurrection Of Our Lord
Easter 2	Easter 2
Easter 3	Easter 3
Easter 4	Easter 4
Easter 5	Easter 5
Easter 6	Easter 6
The Ascension Of Our Lord	The Ascension Of Our Lord
Easter 7	Easter 7
The Day Of Pentecost	The Day Of Pentecost
The Holy Trinity	The Holy Trinity
Proper 4/Pentecost 2/O T 9*	Proper 9
Proper 5/Pent 3/O T 10	Proper 10
Proper 6/Pent 4/O T 11	Proper 11
Proper 7/Pent 5/O T 12	Proper 12
Proper 8/Pent 6/O T 13	Proper 13
Proper 9/Pent 7/O T 14	Proper 14
Proper 10/Pent 8/O T 15	Proper 15
Proper 11/Pent 9/O T 16	Proper 16
Proper 12/Pent 10/O T 17	Proper 17
Proper 13/Pent 11/O T 18	Proper 18
Proper 14/Pent 12/O T 19	Proper 19
Proper 15/Pent 13/O T 20	Proper 20
Proper 16/Pent 14/O T 21	Proper 21
Proper 17/Pent 15/O T 22	Proper 22
Proper 18/Pent 16/O T 23	Proper 23
Proper 19/Pent 17/O T 24	Proper 24
Proper 20/Pent 18/O T 25	Proper 25
Proper 21/Pent 19/O T 26	Proper 26
Proper 22/Pent 20/O T 27	Proper 27
Proper 23/Pent 21/O T 28	Proper 28
Proper 24/Pent 22/O T 29	Proper 29
Proper 25/Pent 23/O T 30	Proper 30
Proper 26/Pent 24/O T 31	Proper 31
Proper 27/Pent 25/O T 32	Proper 32
Proper 28/Pent 26/O T 33	Proper 33
Christ The King (Proper 29/O T 34)	Proper 34/Christ The King/ Reign Of Christ
Reformation Day (October 31)	Reformation Day (October 31)
All Saints (November 1 or 1st Sunday in November)	All Saints' Day (November 1)
Thanksgiving Day (4th Thursday of November)	Thanksgiving Day (2nd Monday of October)

*O T = Ordinary Time

www.ingramcontent.com/pod-product-compliance
Lightning Source LLC
Chambersburg PA
CBHW061249040426
42444CB00010B/2312